I AM GOING
THEN KILL THE CLONE AND EAT IT

writings from 2007-2009

you are walking past
a cemetery, and you
think, "oh yeah, that's right."

ALSO BY SAM PINK

No One Can Do Anything Worse To You Than You Can

The No Hellos Diet

Hurt Others

Person

The Self-Esteem Holocaust Comes Home

Frowns Need Friends Too

I AM GOING TO CLONE MYSELF
THEN KILL THE CLONE AND EAT IT
I AM GOING TO CLONE MYSELF
THEN KILL THE CLONE AND EAT IT
I AM GOING TO CLONE MYSELF
THEN KILL THE CLONE AND EAT IT
I AM GOING TO CLONE MYSELF
THEN KILL THE CLONE AND EAT IT
I AM GOING TO CLONE MYSELF
THEN KILL THE CLONE AND EAT IT
I AM GOING TO CLONE MYSELF
THEN KILL THE CLONE AND EAT IT
I AM GOING TO CLONE MYSELF
THEN KILL THE CLONE AND EAT IT
I AM GOING TO CLONE MYSELF
THEN KILL THE CLONE AND EAT IT

SAM PINK

Lazy Fascist Press
Portland, Oregon

Lazy Fascist Press
An Imprint of Eraserhead Press
205 NE Bryant Street
Portland, Oregon 97211

www.lazyfascistpress.com

ISBN: 978-1-62105-027-8

Cover design by Matthew Revert
www.matthewrevert.com

Interior layout by Cameron Pierce

Printed in the USA.

TABLE OF CONTENTS

TODAY I HOPE A BUS ACCIDENTALLY KILLS ME

Today I hope a bus accidentally kills me. That way, people will look back on everything I did in my life and think about how special it was, because a bus accidentally killed me. The driver wouldn't have to feel bad, because it'd be an accident. And if for some reason the collision didn't kill me, when the driver got out of the bus to check on me, I'd say, "Could you please roll over my head and finish me. I'm in pain and I want to become a hero." People nearby would see the big wheel of the bus smashing my skull into the concrete—my screaming mouth the last thing to go.

I AM THE BEST THING EVER
INTRODUCED TO THE MATERIAL WORLD

Sometimes I don't eat dinner because I'm worried someone will kill me if I leave my room.

I wish there was a cord attached to my forehead that I could pull to raze my skull like one of those collapsible puppets.

When I get home tonight I will close my eyes in the doorway and walk to my room with my eyes closed and go to bed and keep my eyes closed until I fall asleep.

If I swallowed your eye you'd see a big pile of undigested leaves, and the leaves would be covered in caterpillars.

If I were immortal I would go to outerspace and float forever.

Earth and space are the daydream of very tired people.

But you know what, I'm awesome.

And I am glad to meet you.

You will be my friend until I say something to you in person that frightens you.

And I don't know anything about anyone but myself, and even

that is uninteresting.

My goal is to interfere with other people as little as possible and be gone from earth without a sound.

ABSOLUTE HUMAN ABOLITION

On the way to the mailbox today, I slipped on some ice and almost hit my eye on a tree branch. Then I regained my balance and continued on. The guy walking behind me laughed. He had every right to laugh because it was funny and he had no tie to the physical pain I could've experienced. However, if I had lost my eye, I would've walked up to him and held him down in the snow—and let the blood from my empty eye socket spill into his laughing mouth. My mail was mostly things about credit cards and coupons I will never use.

SHORT PLAY

A pizza delivery person stands at the front door of someone's house. He goes to knock again but then hears someone undoing the lock. A man opens the door.

Pizza delivery person: Here you are sir. It's fourteen eighty five.

MAN: [taking the pizza] Uh, ok. Hold on [reaches for his wallet] Uh, do you want to come in? You can come in if you want. I'll give you some of my pizza here and we can watch tv or something—whatever you like to do. I have board games.

PIZZA DELIVERY PERSON: [stops chewing gum and squints at the man] What?

MAN: Yeah. Come on in.

[The pizza delivery guys pops a bubble. Then he is quiet.]

MAN: [softly] Please. Please stay. We can talk or I can make you laugh maybe. Come on–please? I'll pay you for the pizza but please stay.

PIZZA DELIVERY PERSON: No thanks sir. That's fourteen eighty five, please.

MAN: [clears his throat] Isn't there anything I can do to get you to please please please stay even for ten minutes. It's so bad in there.

PIZZA DELIVERY PERSON: There is nothing you can do to get me to stay. Please pay sir. [then slowly] There is nothing you can do to get me to stay—nothing.

MAN: [looks at the pizza box] That's what I thought.

MOVE IN WITH ME

Move in with me. I'm lonely. We can watch television together. We'll laugh at people who make funny observations. When you get hungry, I'll make you food. You'll say, "Man, I could go for…" and I'll make it. I'll put little pieces of glass in the food. Your mouth will flood with blood. You'll tell me something that happened to you during the day and every word will sound pathetic coming through your swollen and cut lips and tongue. I'll say, "Don't talk with your mouth full, it makes you look impolite." You'll put your head in my lap after we eat and I'll put my hands over your face and touch it. My hands will feel heavy on your face. You'll get really uncomfortable and ask to take a shower to clean the feeling off. We'll take a shower together and I'll pinch your ass. You'll laugh. I'll let myself slip to the floor of the shower. The water will roam your back and slip from your ass and hit me in the face. I'll drink the water before it enters the drain. There will be a lot of hair clogging the drain. I'll take it out and put it on my lips like a goatee and I'll act like a middle-aged man who has a goatee. I'll wear sandals and a shirt that says the name of a town in Mexico. I'll kiss you on the lips with my goatee. When you leave the shower, you'll turn the faucet to cold and my heart will hiccup. I'll feel afraid. I'll follow you into my room. While you're toweling off, I'll lock the door and say, "Pray to your god, it's time to suffer. I want to make you level-eyed with my nightmare." Then I'll pause before saying, "Just kidding." I'll jump on the bed naked. You'll say, "Your balls look funny." I'll say, "Like 'Family Circus' funny or what?" Then we'll have sex. When we're done, I'll clean myself off with some tissue paper and the tissue paper will stick to me. I'll hop around the room like a white-tailed deer. You'll put on an orange coat and paint your face with camouflage. You'll say, "Come here little deer, I won't hurt you." Then you'll shoot me in the neck and there will be a huge hole in my neck and the blood will leak into my throat. And we'll sit back down, because between every action there is quiet. "Paint my toes," you'll eventually say, your voice sounding way too loud against the quiet. I'll hold your feet in my hands and paint your toes. I'll feel like crushing the bones. I'll say, "You have nice feet, would you mind if I crushed them with a hammer or a dumbbell." You'll laugh and ask me to turn off the lights so we can sleep. I'll turn off the lights and lie down next to you. You'll fall asleep faster than me and it will rain. The rain will beat the window. I'll open the window and hold out a glass. When the glass is full, I'll drink it. I'll put on some of your lipstick and spit all over my groin. I'll kiss the wall and punch the lipstick stain. I'll feel like obliterating myself. I'll feel like going outside and drowning in a puddle. Just lying down and resting. I'll put some old leaves underneath my eyelids. And the weight of the sky will crush me into rest. I'll wish for this in painful quiet. In painful quiet I'll wish for you to wake up so I won't be alone. But you'll sleep and I'll wait, hoping to be relieved—if only for a second—of the mounting weight that wipes its feet at my door every night.

MANNEQUINS THAT SWEAT BLACK INK
AND NEVER HAVE ANY FUN

I hunt bugs with a miniature bow made of twigs, and arrows fashioned from the creases in your face that represent every time you have frowned.

I am in a retirement home and I am sleeping underneath the bed of an old man who doesn't know who he is anymore and who thinks his family has disappeared. And I keep saying, "Tick tock tick tock, nobody loves you and I won't hold your hand when you die."

If you put red licorice in your ear it looks like your ear is vomiting blood.

If I ever have kids it will be a mistake. And I will apologize to the largest number of people willing to listen.

I wish I were the person you imagine yourself to be because then you'd love me and never let me go.

Lie down; it's time for me to walk over you and call you a bridge I no longer need.

I love everyone who reads this.

AN INCOMPLETE LIST OF THE THINGS I'D LIKE TO BE REINCARNATED AS

A band-aid with a little bit of blood on it and the blood has become brown from being old.

An old man who never dies.

The wind that dried the words in your mouth before you said them—when we were on a walk and thinking about hating each other.

A kite stuck in a tree at six p.m. on an October afternoon with enough wind necessary to constantly push the kite against the tree but not free it.

The blood trapped in your muscles when they clench during an orgasm.

The heat in your mouth.

A body of water filled with skeletons floating like ice cubes—and only the first few feet below the surface allows any sun so the rest is a color no one's ever seen.

An eyelash of yours that falls to the sidewalk then blows into a discarded aluminum can.

A dog that doesn't worry about anything and just eats garbage all day (and also maybe fucks some other homeless dogs too because eating garbage would suck).

The very end of all your laughs.

The fold of skin that collects the most dirt on your body.

A large hill upon which someone you love loses their breath and dies—facedown in the grass.

Myself, because I'll never be done.

APARTMENT

Every time I come home I stand in the doorway and say,
"It's time for a monster to eat me now."

Then it does.

When I go to bed and pull the covers open I say,
"It's time for a monster to eat me now."

Then it does.

Every time I get out of bed I say,
"It's time for a monster to eat me now."

Then it does.

Every time I leave my apartment I say,
"It's time for a monster to eat me now."

Then it does.

ROLLER HOCKEY

When I was ten I used to play roller hockey with the kid who lived across the street. One time his dad came out while we were playing and he got in goal. He said he used to play hockey and that we didn't know what we were doing. Then he asked me to get my dad "out 'ere, and see ifee can man-up." I told him my dad was at work. Then he tried to show me how to hold my stick the right way. His breath smelled like whiskey. He kept pushing me. He said, "That's what hockey is about." Five minutes later, his son and I decided we didn't want to play hockey anymore and that we'd rather swim in the pool in his backyard. As we walked to the pool, the dad said, "Hey, don't be pissin in my pool. Arright? I wouldn't swim in your toilet so don't be pissin in my pool." Later on, while pissing in his pool, I thought to myself, "I wouldn't mind if he swam in my toilet because then it would be easy for me to shit on him. Real easy."

I ENVY THE MOON BECAUSE
IT NEVER HAS TO FACE THE DAY

When I put my ear against your stomach, I hear a storm.

When I put my eyelashes by your tongue and blink real fast, you get a horrified look on your face and I say, "There is a spider tap-dancing on your tongue and I hope you are comfortable because right now will never be over."

And if you pray with your eyes closed real tight, god will make sure no one cuts your legs off.

I lie on the floor and roll over everything that I encounter and when I encounter something I can't roll over, I sleep next to it and hold its eyes shut until it thinks it has died.

Each new relationship is made of cotton and I am a bee that is on fire, lost and ready to land.

And my head is a broken toy.

I hate my head.

And if you don't hate yourself, no one will.

And your broken skull is not a puzzle, it's just garbage.

So be ugly for me or I will hammer a nail into your ear.

You're pathetic and I draw the world on your face before I step on it.

I put the shit that comes out of your mouth beneath your nose.

I sit in my room and cut circles out of the dark and throw them beneath you, hoping hoping hoping hoping hoping that you will fall somewhere I don't even know about, somewhere I couldn't even reach my hand into if I wanted.

Because you are afraid to die.

Because you haven't begun to make it necessary yet.

Because your whole life is a fucking coloring book.

Please change your mind.

I was here first.

MOST PEOPLE ARE NOT
AS GOOD AS ME

A sunburned homeless man came up to me yesterday and showed me his forearm. There was a gaping wound along the bone, barely held together by office staples. The wound leaked clear liquid. I gave him what was in my pockets—70 cents. That was probably enough to buy more staples. Enough to keep his wound somewhat cured. And me? I'm so great it hurts.

HELP ME

I would like to cut off the fingers from my right hand and replace them with all pinky fingers. I would wave the fingers and my hand would look like an underwater plant. I am willing to pay up to five hundred dollars to have this done by a relatively competent doctor or finger expert or even someone who knows what an underwater plant looks like, so they could be like, "Yes" or "No, that doesn't look like an underwater plant."

IF YOU WERE MY BLOOD
I'D OVERDOSE ON HEROIN

I'm sorry.

I didn't want to be at your place when my head broke into pieces all over the floor, spreading out over your tile.

And I didn't want for you to have to watch me clean it up— slowly—big pieces first, then the smaller ones.

I'm sorry.

But if you look at things a certain way, you are always on top of the Earth's curve. And someone is saying "ta-da" wherever you go, but no one is clapping. And that's good because clapping is the sound of things going wrong.

I'm going to smash your arms and legs and pour the dust into an hourglass and measure how long it takes me to forget that I'm one of billions of people who showed up to the party uninvited and with nothing in their hands.

I'm sorry.

VOLUNTARY DEATH

At the post office I saw an old man sitting in his wheelchair. His face was a very slow waterfall. A little girl walked up to him and tugged on his sleeve and asked him a question. As he answered, he drooled into his lap. He drooled a long glassy cord. Then he wiped his mouth with an American flag handkerchief tucked underneath the collar of his shirt. The little girl said, "Ewww" and walked away.

SELFISH ASSHOLE

You're mean. You didn't leave your window unlocked last night. You didn't leave your window unlocked and I couldn't come into your house. I couldn't give you kisses while you were sleeping. And I couldn't sit in your dark room and feel like the darkness was dyeing my skin. I couldn't pull the blanket over your exposed leg, and pat the blanket down and say, "There you go." And I couldn't take a shower and use your apricot-cucumber soap and see my pubes stick to the bar. I couldn't put my mouth over your cat's head and just stand there while it scratched my face. And I couldn't put little bombs in between your teeth. I couldn't split you down the middle with a box cutter and get inside and hang a picture that says, "Home is inside the person you kind of hate and have sliced open with a box cutter." And I couldn't clip my fingernails and secrete the clippings somewhere behind your couch in the hopes that another me would grow and relieve me of my responsibility to you. I couldn't pick off a scab and put it in your strawberry jelly (because if there's one person I want to eat my scabs, it's you baby, it's you). And I couldn't sit by your bed and shove a flower into your ear so you'd finally look pretty. I couldn't lift your leg and put my head beneath and constantly drop your leg so it looks like you're kicking me. And I couldn't lift your arm and see your armpit hair grow. I couldn't push my face into your armpit hair and pretend like I was at a carwash. And I definitely couldn't make some tea and then throw it at your sleeping face and say, "Here's some tea, just how you like it." I couldn't ultimately decide that I wanted to run back outside. And I couldn't climb back out the window and look for another window. Because someone is always going to leave their window open for me.

PUBIC HAIR THAT IS
HARD WITH BLOOD

I would like to blow up my left eye with a small firecracker.

I would like the firecracker to be large enough to totally explode my eye, but small enough to leave the rest of my head intact (maybe just blacken the socket a little).

I am the process of billions of years of motion and the predecessor of billions more.

And the grass along the sidewalk in front of my apartment is green during the day and black at night and I am always the same.

Look at the dirt on my face and I will look at the dirt on your face and we will never stop having a very painful orgasm.

I would like to camp out in one of your pores. And set up a scaffold on your face and keep it clean. You wouldn't have to pay me anything. I would wash your face with my tongue and hopefully a small mop of some sort (or ideally, a small mop made of tongues).

I would also like to rub my face against the carpet until I expose my skull. But I almost never do the things I want.

My only goal is to destroy myself and everything else.

And I spend at least five minutes out of every hour fantasizing about my bones breaking. (Usually my fingers).

I'm on the sun trying to extinguish it with my spit. I spit into the ocean and make it bigger.

My hands are numb after sleeping on them and I am pressing them into your head. It will be ok if my fingers break when I push them into your head because I won't feel it.

And the organs in my body would feel cheated if they knew the result of their work. This is an apology to my organs.

The sun is inside all the plants you eat and the animals that eat them and something will eat you and something will eat me. This is a promise.

Smell me. I am at least 1/3 dead.

Come to my room and get on your hands and knees and I will sleep on your back while you crawl around on the floor. We can take turns.

I am going to make a wig out of the dust that covers the floor. I will put the wig on my pillow and hug my pillow and be nice to my pillow.

My sink is full of dead flies and I don't empathize with anyone.

The price of every friendship is loss of time.

Having friends is narcissistic.

Climb onto your roof and yell at everyone that passes. You are safe on the roof.

I used a net to catch some bugs and I put the bugs into my mouth and whispered them into your ear.

And you didn't hear what I said.

And you learned that wherever you take your stand, your back is turned on something else.

In the shower I cross my arms and let the water collect on the inside of my elbows and then the hairs on my arm sway in slow, underwater-motion and I imagine myself as a plankton with no hope or intention, navigating the hairs and hating the ground beneath me.

I am going to collect the eyes from all the dead animals and bugs I find and tape them to my eyes and kaleidoscope the world.

My spine is frozen spit and I dare you to break it in half.

Tonight I will know what I learned today and tomorrow I will forget it and learn it again.

SEVEN VERSIONS
OF THE SAME VERSION

1.

I sat next to an old man on the bus yesterday. Our legs touched. We sat still for miles. A girl walked by us at a stop. The old man watched her pass then nudged me. He motioned for me to look too.

"Whew, huh?" he said. Then he turned and smiled at me.

I tried to think of something to say.

"Yeah I know," I said. "I'd definitely love to bite off one of her eyebrows and glue it to my upperlip. I've always wanted a pretty moustache. Or you know, just microwave a bowl of her blood— see what happens."

He readjusted himself in his seat and we sat staring forward for the remainder of the ride.

2.

The girl passed by and the old man elbowed me to look.

"Man, how bout it huh?" he said.

I smiled and nodded. Then I spoke loudly. "Yes, I agree with what I think you are suggesting. I would love to have sex with that girl. I don't know who she is but I think we can both agree that we should think about her body. I am aroused. How about you. Are you aroused, sir. Let's think about what we'd do. Let's think together. We can holds hands if you want, but that's up to you."

3.

The girl passes us and the old man puts his head in his hands. His head bounces in his lap with each subsequent turn and bump in the road.

4.

The girl passes us. As she passes, she temporarily blocks the window I've been watching, and the field outside it. I am angry that now I remember I am on a bus going somewhere and this somewhere will probably require something of me and I will either know or not know how to do that something and whoever is there, if even just me, will judge me capable or incapable. I'm now upset.

5.

The girl passes and leaves the bus and walks down the street and I never see her again. She will not think about me as she walks down the street into the millions of paths we will never choose in accord.

6.

I am almost asleep when the bus rounds a corner and sunlight comes through the window. The man next to me becomes rigid. He points to the cube-shaped piece of light on my shirt.

"Shit," he says loudly. "Oh shit. Get it off, quick." He leans back, pointing. The cube on my shirt grows. "Get it off—it's on you—get it off. Oh shit."

He crawls backwards to avoid the sunlight. I lose sight of him as the cube covers my face and I become too comfortable to stay awake.

"It's all over you—move," he yells. "Please."

His yells become more like pathetic whining and the whining sounds wet coming from the muscles in his throat.

The girl walking by is just one part of an endless number of things.

7.

I ignore the man and the girl. I feel a steady ringing begin in my ears. I am conscious of the ringing. It is all I can sense. It quiets my steps as I get off the bus. Somehow, I know it is my stop. I walk home. Somehow, I know all the steps. Someone is walking thirty feet or so behind me. I am afraid they are going to kill me. I am afraid but I shouldn't be, because no one would want to kill me. I repeat this to myself. "Don't be afraid. They're not going to kill you." I try to put the keys in my door quickly. The apartment is dark. I sit on my couch and worry about things that are not present. I let revolve in my head all the things I have to do, ultimately doing none of them until I begin to feel sleepy. I go to my room and lock the door. Halfway through the night, I wake up. I don't fall back asleep. Instead, I watch with eyes half-closed as the window in my room becomes lighter. It is almost time to get back on the bus.

CULTURE IS STUPID

I am watching you sleep and repeating the words, "You are my enemy" over and over until the steam collects on your face and your pores turn the steam into icicles of a whole new kind of sharpness.

Shake hands with your enemy to test their bones.

I am 24.

Living another 50 years seems impossible.

RESOLUTION

If I ever decide to shoot myself, I'll make sure to stuff my mouth with confetti, so it looks pretty for no one.

MY CAREER

I used to have an eight pack of crayons.
Then I bought a sixteen pack.
Then there were too many colors and I ran out of corresponding emotions.

Everybody likes me but that's because I'm a mirror lying face down in an empty field.

You know you're truly alone when you feel the need to tell someone about a nap you recently took.
You know there is nothing to say so let's take a nap.

And I am pissing on your grave.
I hope your mouth is open for this.

Today I will waste so much time the orbit of the earth will loosen, jettisoning our planet to freezing depths, far from the sun.
And I will not regret it.

I will claim you as my own, when everyone else disclaims you.
And I will not regret it.

And flies will eat your dead body.

My ideal date would involve painful silence.
My ideal date wouldn't involve me.

Nail me to your wall and I will make a sad face while I watch you sleep.
I will give you a goodnight kiss but it will feel gross to you.
And I will not regret it.

Sometimes I wish I were a hair on your body because then I could be close to you but not have to say anything.
And sometimes I wish you were a hair on my body so I could cut you with a razor and not get in trouble.

All day I can only hear what sounds like a small annoyed kid playing a keyboard at a department store.

And if you find my skeleton in the forest, feel free to crack my ribcage in half and use the halves to rake up the dead leaves then burn them and smell the burn and say something you definitely don't mean.

I will pull patches of hair out of my head just like plants from dirt prepared by heavy rainfall.
And I'll call it maintenance because my field must remain undeveloped.
Because hair is bad ideas coming out of the skull.

There are too many emotions.
But I really only feel one, and it's, "I would kiss you goodnight except I'm allergic to assholes."

Outside of my head there is someone thinking, "Outside of my head there is someone thinking, 'Outside of my head there is someone thinking.'"

And your opinion never bruises me, it tickles.

All my fingers are criminals.

Only as beautiful as the worst thing I've done.

Personal eugenic scrutiny.
When the world holds its breath, I take mine.

I am the last breath of everyone you have loved.
I leave their body and blend with wind.
When I move, I flip over a leaf and an ant falls off the tip and slides down a wet blade of grass.

I set out little pieces of glass because I want the people who chase me to feel the trail beneath them.
I have no friends that have survived all circumstances.

I am good in bed (at sleeping).
Watch me sleep and see me wake up looking ungrateful.
I look at the ceiling and think, "There is no way to leave here."
And I am always right.

You are everything that you hide.
And I hug you to see behind you.
Or maybe to crush some vital organ.

This kind of scare is the worst.
This kind of scare involves us both forgetting everything.
This kind of scare makes us into confused people.
Both convinced we owe each other something.
But instead we become one aimless person.

And today, I have nothing to say and am proud of my decision not to try and come up with something.
I am waiting for whatever is mine.
It is better that way.
I have measured myself for the last few weeks and nothing has changed.
It is better that way.

I feel holy.

Somewhere in space is my first breath.

And you will become the people you hate.
You will remember them by becoming them.
Or no, you will become them by remembering them.
Their faces are little shields that prevent everyone else from becoming important to you.

WHAT I AM THINKING RIGHT NOW

I wonder if the man in front of me in line at the post office has any clue that I have been considering how many times I would have to stab the back of his skull with my pen, to break through and see his brain.

CONVERSATION

My friend and I went to a Chinese buffet for dinner. We sat at a table next to another table where a man with a smashed-looking face sat in a wheelchair—by himself—with a plate of rice scattered before him. He moaned loudly at random intervals.

"Man, shit's good," my friend said, clipping off a noodle with his teeth.

"Yeah," I said. "You should've told me it was ten dollars though. You said six before."

He laughed a little. "Sorry man, I forgot." Then he looked around, at the lamps, the mirrors, the greeter, and the man in the wheelchair. "I got some good fucking food like this in Thailand when I was stationed there."

I said, "Oh yeah?"

He nodded and rubbed his nose.

The man in the wheelchair moaned.

"Yeah," my friend said. "But shit is fucked up there, man. People fucking five-year-olds and shit." He turned and chewed, and surveyed the restaurant again. He spoke as if to himself. "At a place like this, you could just walk in and fuck a toddler. That simple.

In the back room"—he snapped his fingers—"Ta-da, you fuck a five-year-old. I'm sure people fuck five-year-olds here too though. But I mean—"

"Probably," I said, reintroducing myself to the conversation.

"Definitely," he said. He put a shrimp in his mouth and chewed a few times before slowing to clarify. "But I mean, yeah, there it's everywhere man. You go into a restaurant like this, and— Presto!—you fuck a five-year-old."

I was becoming increasingly more impressed with his use of magician vernacular to introduce the ease of fucking a five-year-old in Thailand.

"I mean, they practically make you fuck a five-year-old there man," he said. "Shit is disgusting." He shivered and looked at the end of his fork.

"Yeah," I said. "Here you have to like, take the five-year-old out and be nice to it and ask it about its dreams and aspirations, make the five-year-old feel comfortable. Fuck that."

The man in the wheelchair moaned and squirmed and a woman came out of the bathroom next to where he was sitting, and walked up to him.

"Ok Gerald, let's go," she said. "We can rent a movie if you want."

I ate a shrimp off my friend's plate. "Those are good," I said.

"Yeah, they're over next to the steamed asparagus."

I said, "In Thailand, did they have like, a bin that said, 'Shrimp' and then one that said, 'Asparagus' and then one that said, 'Toddlers to fuck.'"

"They don't speak English in Thailand, you dumb fuck," he said.

The man in the wheelchair moaned and screamed as the woman put a wet paper towel up to his face and wiped the rice and sauce off his chin. The rice pelted the table and ground, dully resonant like rain hitting a tent.

"Stop squirming Gerald," she said. "Or no movie."

UNTITLED

I must be a piece of dust because I make your eyes water and you always try to get rid of me but I'm always coming back.

TOMORROW IS ON FIRE
AND I AM VERY YOUNG

Tomorrow is on fire and I am very young. Tomorrow I press your face into the ash of the old bridge. Tomorrow I push the ash of the old bridge into your eyes. Tomorrow I hate everyone I've ever heard of or known. Tomorrow is on fire and I am still very young. Tomorrow I will return and I am not a vindictive person, but I will point my finger in your face repeatedly, and my fingernail will make little moons on your face. The pressure will create little bruises around the moons, little clouds. Tomorrow is on fire and I am very young. You don't have to remember any of this, because I will keep saying it.

OUR MAIDEN NAME

First I produce a meaningful moment in your life then stop communicating with you so you feel hurt.

Then I do it as many times in a row as I can.

I can recite many things about myself that are true—like my address, name, and phone number.

Sometimes I recite these things to make sure I haven't become a completely different person.

But mostly I'm a cripple turning rusty padlocks.

Not one of them yet has opened to anything but another rusty padlock.

Here comes the creep of sun through my window again.

Which means I have to act like a human again.

Which means it's time to turn into a rusty padlock again.

There is no one to talk to and nothing to see.

Sleep tight.

I LIKE BEING AT THE LIBRARY

Today at the library, I walked up to someone sleeping in a chair. I gently shook her. She looked up at me through the hair covering her face. I put my hand on her forehead and said, "My child, you will not be forgotten by me, your holy father, the one who loves you and cleans you with the fleece of his chosen lambs. You will know my infinite love. And can I borrow eighty cents so I can buy some chips from that vending machine over there, please."

ADVICE

A good thing to say after shaking someone's hand is: "Finally. I have always wanted to touch another human."

Another good thing to say is: "I will never be clean again" while looking idly at your hand.

THING THAT DETAILS A TRIP TO THE SUPERMARKET

Yesterday I went to the supermarket to buy groceries. Buying groceries causes me much dread because it is always the same. I buy the same things. I walk in the same direction. I eat the same foods and leave the packages in the same places. And I show my genitals to the same employees.

I borrowed my friend's car and drove to the supermarket. I grabbed a cart and went to the produce aisle. I eat a lot of fruit so that's usually where I start. Plus, listening to the sprayers calms me down enough so I don't have a stroke and die on the floor in front of a little kid playing a handheld videogame while his mom scratches things off a list.

One of the things I hate about the supermarket is the feeling that everyone is looking at me. It makes me feel like someone who is severely handicapped, who you put up with because you're afraid he'll lose his temper and hurt you badly.

I went to the cantaloupe section and looked at the cantaloupes. I surveyed the cantaloupes and picked one up. I smelled it and decided it was the one for me.

"You are mine," I said to the cantaloupe. "Don't fight it. It will be easier if you just come along with me. I will provide a home for you and you will grow to love me. You will call me father. Just relax and be cool and you won't get hurt."

I put the cantaloupe in the cart and went to the avocado section. A middle-aged woman pulled her cart up to the avocados too and we stood there looking at them. I touched one and it was soft.

The woman said, "Are they any good today?"

I said, "I don't know, I—"

"Usually they're soft," she said, pressing her finger into one.

"Like my spirit," I said.

She grabbed one and walked away and so did I. I went to the dried fruit section and saw a bag that read, "Island Mix."

"Come sail away," I said, and put the bag in my cart, with no emotion on my face.

I pushed the cart to the next aisle and almost ran into two girls who were shopping together. I felt uncomfortable about walking past them so I stood behind them and acted like I was checking out products. I noticed the brand name oatmeal cost twice as much as the generic kind.

I turned to the old lady behind me and said, "Man check out those motherfucking savings. Those are the motherfuckingest savings I've ever seen."

The two girls in front of me walked on, and I kept inching up behind them. We'd unfortunately chosen similar paths at similar times. It became very entertaining.

Who will break first, I thought.

I had two options.

Rather than kill them, I went to the next aisle over and then went backwards after that, to disrupt what would have been a crippling repetition of encounters.

I'm brilliant, I thought.

I checked out the bread section. I grabbed a loaf then noticed the bag was ripped. I put it back quickly and looked around to make sure no one saw me and blamed me. There was an old man behind me.

Play it cool, I thought. He didn't see shit. Everything is fine. If he starts talking, just push him down and bang his head against the tile until he is silent. No one's going to fucking catch you. Not ever.

The old man came up to me and said, "Excuse me, where's the celery at around here?"

I pulled a butterfly knife out of my pants and shoved it into his eye and screamed at his dying body.

No, I didn't do that. I just lied to you. I'm sorry.

I pointed toward the produce section and said, "The celery is that way."

He said something like, "Well alright goddamn it. Finally, some answers."

In the same aisle as the bread was the peanut butter. This will keep me from dying, I thought, and put a jar into my cart.

I went to the frozen food aisle and looked at the frozen vegetables. I wanted some peas. I found the peas. There were many different bags. One of the bags said, "Fancy Sweet Peas."

No, I thought. Then I contrived a sad look at the floor while idly kicking at the tile. Those aren't for me. I am not worth it. Maybe one day, but not today. Not fancy peas. Only regular peas. I will stay humble. Fancy peas will only lead to the inception of a progressively grander ideal of life. Where will it end.

I was walking back with a bag of normal peas in my hand when I noticed someone walking by my cart at the other end of the aisle.

Try it motherfucker, I thought. Try to steal that shit. I'm begging you. Test providence. How are we going to do this? Huh?

The person walked closer to my cart.

Oh hell no, I thought. Hell fuck-ing no. I worked too hard assembling all that shit for you to just steal it. Over my fucking dead body.

I started to take off my coat and then calmed down as the person walked by me and smiled.

Lucky. You're lucky motherfucker. Must be a fucking angel watching over you. Next time, we'll see. God can't watch forever.

At the end of the aisle there was another full cart. I thought about taking it. I'd always wanted to steal a full cart and just push it somewhere else. No one would expect that. It would totally ruin their day. All that hard work undone. Gone. Vanished. The sorrow.

I went to the juice aisle and saw some Apple Strawberry Banana juice.

Oh yes, I thought. It's fucking party time. This is for me. I deserve this. It's time to treat myself. This will add joy to my life. This is for me.

I heard someone walking behind me say, "Well, you said you needed this goddamn celery, now I got it, and you say you don't need it. What the hell. Yes or no. I'm telling you now to make up your goddamn mind."

A woman said, "Keep it down, Harold."

"Yeah keep it down Harold," I said, and then pulled out a shotgun and blasted my head against a box of cereal with a surfing kangaroo on the front.

No, I didn't do that. I lied again. I won't lie again.

I put the juice in my cart and went to the check out lane.

The guy at the register asked me how I was doing.

I said, "I feel great—like I'm on heroin and getting my dick sucked by three girls at once."

He rang me up.

I said, "I will pay you fifty dollars to cut my head off with an axe."

He asked me if I wanted a bag for the gallon of milk.

"You're my gallon of milk baby," I said.

He said, "Stop being such a stupid asshole."

I apologized.

Then I left the store.

On the drive home I heard a song on the radio. In the song, a guy sang, "Ah'm so addicted to you."

This song would only be cool if it were about methamphetamines, or maybe cake, I thought.

Then I turned the radio off.

GENITAL MUTILATION

In middle school, a kid in my class fastened a sharpened pencil to one of those rectangular pink erasers and set it on some other kid's seat. The other kid sat on the pencil and the pencil punctured his scrotum. He told us about it the next week when he came back to school. I didn't get a chance to ask him if one or both of his balls fell out (it was only later that I found out your balls are attached to something).

A PARTIAL LIST OF THINGS
I FEEL LIKE RIGHT NOW

A wrinkled hot dog spinning under a lightbulb in a gas station.

A pair of shoes stuck on an electrical wire.

The smell of a cough that an old man with lung cancer coughs into his hands.

Something important that was written on a chalkboard and then erased and you can still kind of see some of it.

A recently shit in diaper with a handful of sprinkles dropped on it.

Absolutely nothing.

SANDCASTLE

Me and you on a beach, the sand of which is my pulverized skeleton. I am making sandcastles with a shattered plastic bucket. I will enter your body and cough black ants with large abdomens into your bloodstream. You will cough the black ants out of your face and they will sink into the dust of my skeleton. The sand is my skeleton and your coughing turns up swirls. On your hands and knees, dead with my fluid, you will act as I made you.

I AM GOING TO JUMP-KICK
YOUR FACE AND THEN KISS IT

I am going to jump-kick your face and then kiss it. I have been practicing my jump-kicks every day. I have been practicing my jump-kicks at least three or four times a day. That means I have performed more jump-kicks than the average human. That means when I jump-kick your face you will notice the power. That means when I jump-kick your face, it will mean more than if someone else did it. After I jump-kick your face I will kiss it. There will be many kisses—an amount that eventually becomes annoying and vaguely frightening. They will seem mad. And I won't even feel emotion while I'm kissing your face. It will just be something I am doing. I will kiss your face repeatedly. Mainly in the cheek area. But sometimes on the nose and sometimes on the forehead. And sometimes my mouth will be open. Sometimes my front teeth will touch your skin and it will be accidental. And I promise to open my eyes to assure you if that happens. When you feel teeth and then open your eyes, mine will already be open. But I will not stop kissing your face. The pleas to stop will not be obeyed. The next day you will wake up with your face against the pillow—your jump-kicked and violently-kissed face. It will hurt. You will touch it and feel how it hurts. I am practicing my jump-kicks—my kisses are already pretty good. You will get one of the former and many of the latter. You mean nothing and you are nobody. You are a crumb in my bellybutton. I am your universe.

I DON'T KNOW ANYTHING
OR CARE ABOUT ANYTHING
AND I SHOULD PROBABLY JUST
SIT IN A FOLDING CHAIR
AND DIE

Videotape your face and let it watch over you as you sleep.

Draw a picture of yourself and eat it.

Don't let culture lay a hand on you.

And don't own anything.

Don't envy anyone.

I put tape over your mouth and bang your head against the wall.

This is the perfect moment entering the perfect idea and vice versa.

Just let it pass.

UGANDAN HOOKER

My old roommate let one of his military buddies move in a while back. When the guy moved in, he spent three months on the living room couch staring at the tv. He ate chips and watched soap operas all day. I had a conversation with him one afternoon. He talked about Uganda where he was previously stationed. He said, "Yeah man, if a hooker gets pregnant there, they make her eat the baby right after it's born." I said, "I wish my mom was a Ugandan hooker."

A PLAY ABOUT TWO PEOPLE

From neighboring houses emerge two men. They walk through their lawns and stand three feet apart. A floodlight on one's driveway strobes on. The air suggests the end of summer.

THE ONE: It's nice to see you. [smiles]

THE OTHER ONE: [matching the smile] Yeah, you too.

They both reach for their pockets. Eyes together. With slow precision they put black-handled steak knives against each other's throats.

THE ONE: I think the summer is gone. I feel the cooling.

THE OTHER ONE: So do I. Soon I'll shut my windows.

THE ONE: Yes, when the cooling comes it is best to shut your windows. It keeps things warm in the house.

THE OTHER ONE: Thank you for the advice. You are a good friend. Unlike the sun, which is now farther away.

THE ONE: Thank you, I try. It makes me feel good.

THE OTHER ONE: Looking at pictures of myself makes me feel good. Sometimes it is good to know I've been a different person before.

THE ONE: Pictures scare me. I don't let people take pictures of me.

THE OTHER ONE: Thank you for telling me that. Now I know more about you.

THE ONE: Please, do not mention it. It's nothing.

THE OTHER ONE: I am happy to live next to you. You are humble and that makes me feel strong because I could beat you to death and you would do nothing. You'd say, "It's nothing."

THE ONE: You're abusing my humbleness and friendship.

THE OTHER ONE: If you don't cut your lawn periodically, the bugs and animals take over.

THE ONE: [breathes out loudly] I know.

A leaf blows between them. The one pushes his knife a little. It pinches a vein on the other one's throat.

THE ONE: It's nice to see you.

THE OTHER ONE: Yeah, you too. I think we've said this before.

THE ONE: When I don't see you for a long time, I think you don't exist anymore.

THE OTHER ONE: Oh, that's so silly.

THE ONE: I was being sincere and now you have insulted me. You might as well beat me to death now because I am nothing anymore.

THE OTHER ONE: Yes, my arms are strong. My jaw is strong too. I could eat you after you're dead—bones and all. My wife tells me I could eat rocks. Sometimes, she puts rocks in my mouth while I'm sleeping and moves my jaw up and down to test her idea. I am usually awake but I pretend to sleep.

THE ONE: You are a good person and a good husband and it is very nice to see you.

There follows a pause in which both men secretly try to push the knives in further, each fearing detection and retaliation. A car drives by and passes down the block and becomes nothing.

THE ONE: Last weekend, I was cooking and my doorbell rang. I froze. Then it rang again. I put my head over the stove and kept my eyes open. The doorbell rang again. My eyelashes melted into my face and my face felt tight. I stood there until the doorbell stopped. I stood there until becoming calm was again an option. When I hear my doorbell I know it is because everyone wants to kill me and people in the town volunteer to try so the town will be better. I know this. Part of me wants to help make the town better but another part of me is naturally afraid to die. Especially in some horrible way, like hit in the head with a baseball bat repeatedly, which is what I'd imagine the town volunteer would do. I figure, they all would probably contribute for a community baseball bat so killing me would be cheap.

An ice cream truck drives by and the song warps.

THE ONE: I enjoy ice cream. I would have just bought some, but if I ate it now, I wouldn't be able to eat dinner and the wife that I don't have would kill me because she is making something nice I bet.

THE OTHER ONE: I enjoy ice cream too. But sometimes I'm worried that while I am eating an ice cream cone the ice cream will go into a hole in my tooth and my tooth will rot and turn gray and fall into my ice cream cone and I will eat it because I think it is a nut. Other than that though, I really like ice cream. A lot.

THE ONE: Sometimes, I watch you swimming in your pool late at night. I know you think that your pool is hidden because it is in the corner of your yard and it is underneath some trees, but I can still see it. I climb the tree in my backyard and sit there and watch you and your wife swimming. She looks nice with her hair wet and flung back. You look nice too. But the way she looks nice seems nicer than the way you look nice. Does that make sense.

THE OTHER ONE: [slowly pulling his knife back along the skin a little, in a sawing motion—small amount of blood crawls over the knife] Yes, that does make sense. It makes sense for a number of reasons. One, because I feel the same way about looking at my wife and two because I have been trying to figure out why there is an enormous cat that looks like you in your tree every night when I am swimming. I thank you for clarifying that. Also, when I said 'a number of reasons' I meant two. And I have provided the two and now I am done.

THE ONE: [swallows, blood goes down in neck in the directions sweat has already traced] One time when I was up in the tree watching you two, I brought some popcorn and I kept saying, "Let's go see a picture show Betty." Even though I knew it wasn't a picture show and even though "picture show" is an anachronism and even though I don't know anyone named Betty.

The one turns the blade slowly and runs the tip along the other one's neck until the tip is pointing straight at the other one's adam's apple.

THE OTHER ONE: Even though you have imaginary friends and you eat popcorn in a tree, I still accept you as a human being.

THE ONE: Thank you. Now please, I have been a hog. Please tell me about yourself. I want to know all about you.

THE OTHER ONE: Well—last night I was peeling an apple and I accidentally cut myself. I just stood there watching the cut. It looked purple underneath the kitchen light. There was a centipede staring at me from the wall. It just stared. I stared back—all the way until morning. By then, the apple was covered in flies. Every few minutes I lifted the apple to see them fly away. I'm not the king—I just watch the kingdom.

The one narrows his eyes. A rabbit runs across their yards. The rabbit goes into a bush. A bush is a mother with a million arms.

THE OTHER ONE: The cooling is coming.

THE ONE: [almost laughs] I know, I feel it.

THE OTHER ONE: Will you lock your door and windows tonight.

THE ONE: It is the only way.

THE OTHER ONE: Yes.

The sky is now dark blue. And the floodlight at the one's house is hung with bugs. The two men lower their knives and walk back through their lawns, shoes capped in wetness. They feel the cooling. They will shut their windows. They will shake their fists quietly, to themselves. The numbers will move on their clocks. They will watch—to make sure things are moving and changing. They will see each other again and again.

DMV THING

At the DMV, while I waited for my new license to be printed, a lady walked in with a stroller. At the same time, I noticed a sign on the wall that read: No Eating or Drinking. I turned to the lady and motioned to her kid. "Excuse me ma'am, read the sign," I said. Then I realized she wasn't going to eat the kid, she was just watching it or whatever. But you never know.

HOLD HANDS WITH SOMEONE WHO HATES YOU

Praise is step one to death.

Don't look at me.

The next time you give birth to me I will curl up and strangle you before I am fully out.

And I encourage you to make my skull into your showerhead.

And I encourage you to enjoy the showerhead.

I'm looking for someone to spend time with.

But I can't afford too many hellos.

I WOULD FEEL BETTER ON EARTH WITHOUT YOU HERE

I should've worn underwear today. I should've called up a random number and asked them to come over today. I should've cut up the newspaper and made up new news today. I shouldn't even acknowledge that today is today. I should buy a model car set and assemble it and put it in my toilet and shit on it today. I should make up my own religion today. I should clean my boots. I should pry loose the slots of dirt from the treads and make a mannequin of myself. I should remember that I am going to die today. Not die today maybe, but remember it today. I should take a picture of myself to make sure I am real today. I should make sure.

I MAKE SHAPES

After I tear you in half I make shapes with your remains—distill salt from your body and use it to kill the plants growing on the better side of who you are—throw rocks at your statue—forget everything about you.

I have made marionettes out of my most painful anxieties and forced them into war and their blood has fed the earth's skin and grown the next war's field.

They'll come again as different shapes saying the same things. They'll come again and tear me in half.

I AM THE DICTATOR

Yesterday, we built a fort together out of a blanket and the couch and a few chairs.

The fort was flimsy but stayed up.

We brought a box of cereal underneath and laughed about how fun it was to be hidden.

We passed the cereal box back and forth and took turns eating it.

You told me a funny joke while I was eating and I purposely spit the cereal out on the floor of our fort.

The joke was: "I'm pregnant."

I swept the cereal back into order and put it back into the box.

The fort became really hot and sweat beaded around your mouth.

I put my fingers by your lips and did a little windshield washer motion.

I did it kind of hard.

Then there was quiet.

We did the wordsearch on the back of the cereal box and I found everything except for "cereal" "happy" and "hippo."

"Pillow fight," I said.

Then I hit you in the face with a pillow.

You laughed.

I said, "If the police come, don't tell them I hit you with a pillow. Tell them you fell, or I'll smash a hot lightbulb in your mouth."

You made a scared face.

"Just kidding," I said, and we laughed because for a second you thought I was actually going to burn your mouth.

I laughed loudly with my mouth wide so you could see my teeth.

Then we rolled around in the fort and laughed some more.

The fort kept coming undone and you kept fixing it.

You were good at fixing it.

We decided that freedom could be a dangerous thing in our fort utopia, so some form of political structure was needed.

I said plutocracy but you countered with dictatorship and I quickly said, "I call dictator."

You shrugged and allowed it because I was the dictator and if you fucked with me, that'd be it.

Our first task was to enact the systematic exclusion of all unwanted elements.

We created death camps.

One for everyone.

We killed everyone.

After the exterminations, you said you felt sleepy, and you lay down on the fort floor and fell asleep.

I put my hand on your stomach and it was warm.

I ate another handful of cereal and pulled out a bunch of plastic bags from my pocket.

I laid the bags out on the floor and straddled you.

I slid my forefinger and middle finger into your mouth along the crease of your tongue.

My fingers felt warm inside.

My stomach and groin tightened.

You continued to breathe and I put my mouth by yours and said, "I am the dictator."

Then I put my whole hand in your mouth and began pushing it down your throat.

Your throat was tight and smooth.

I got hard.

I kept my hand narrow.

The hairs on my hand and wrist slicked back and your throat bulged with my arm.

I pulled my hand back out with your heart in my hand.

I put it into a plastic bag.

I continued with the rest of your organs and your chest and abdomen sank in and grew wrinkled.

I did not find what I was looking for.

I sat back and touched each of the bags, wanting to see every little cell that beat life into you.

Wanting to take each organ to the sink in the bathroom and wipe all the blood off and trace the grooves with my fingers, pull back flaps and put my fingers in valves.

Smell them.

Know their shape and how they keep you alive to smile, or say something annoying.

Then I thought about filling up a leaf blower with nails and destroying each of the organs.

Would a leaf blower filled with nails do that, I thought. Would a leaf blower filled with nails kill organs.

I knew that inside your body there was something else.

I put my hands into the skin of your stomach like I was diving.

Then I pulled back two flaps and exposed your insides.

There was black water and leaves and twigs and little water-skipping bugs.

The black water drained and revealed a small body.

The arms were undeveloped, like featherless wings and the head resembled a bird-skull.

It was already dead when I scooped it out.

Sometimes you just have to relieve something of its surroundings for it to die.

I cradled the body and left the fort to the sound of your hollow breathing.

My shirt stuck to my belly with sweat.

I brought the body outside and set it in the alley, where the raccoons lived.

It was dark already.

I wiped my hands on my pants.

"I am the dictator," I said.

THE PRETTY MUCH DEAD LION

Today I walked to the library wearing shoes but no socks. By the time I got to the library, my heels and toes were bleeding. The library was closed. So I took my shoes off and sat on the steps for a while. Then I walked to the gas station across the street and bought some coffee and took a few napkins too. I sat on the curb outside and drank my coffee and wrapped pieces of the napkins around my bleeding toes. The wind blew against the blood-stained tissues and the tissues waved. They were my flags and I sat on the curb feeling like a very old lion with gray hairs on his face, not sure if he's even hungry enough to kill anything anymore.

PICNIC

In high school I was invited to a picnic at a forest preserve. Halfway there, I realized I had forgotten to purchase anything to bring to the picnic so I pulled over on the side of the road and grabbed a dead raccoon. I picked it up by the tail. All the hair stripped clean and it fell back to the ground. There were maggots crawling out of its ass. I left the raccoon where I found it and brought conversation and joviality to the picnic instead.

YESTERDAY

Yesterday I walked by a Chicago Police Department Training Headquarters. Three cops were walking down the sidewalk and one of them was gesturing to the others like he was cleaning the inside of a glass. I heard him say, "Yeah, the guy was like, 'What's that sound?' and then I was like, 'Relax, I'm putting your brain back in.'"

I SMASH MY SMILE
AGAINST YOURS

And I fill my mouth with mud and put broken sticks in the mud and while you watch tv I bite you and bruise your arms and leave my name and address by the bruises so people know who gave them to you.

And I climb up trees and look out across fields and I feel fine eating candy by myself in a room and I have no ideas at all and I spit onto the sidewalk sometimes and watch ants eat it.

And I laugh at almost everything and your intestines are my umbilical cord and my umbilical cord is burnt shut and I am laughing right now and my laughing is my umbilical cord.

And I will hold your hand but I will have covered my palm in purple magic-marker so it makes it look like your hand is completely bruised.

And I smash my smile against yours and I'm not going to remember anything that happened today.

And I like to make out with the lines in your forehead when you frown at me.

And I want someone to think I am great for three seconds.

And I masturbate into the toilet and watch the clumps float like ghosts.

And I made my hand into a hospital and I made a replica of your heart out of mud and now I am going to fix it.

And I feel embarrassed for long periods of time without knowing why and there are a lot of pubes around the rim of my toilet and I am starting to feel overrated as a human.

And I am a headless bird in the park on the cold, wet grass, and today the minutes pass me in slow, parade-float indifference.

And I only like things that have been beaten to death then resurrected.

And I put my head through the wall and fall asleep standing up.

And I want to break everything you own and then sit by the broken things and wait for you to return and when you do, I'll be like, "Yeah, I did all of this, how's it going."

And I hope you live for a hundred years so it takes you a hundred years to die.

And I never say hello to someone unless they already said hello to me and sometimes I act so nice to people it frightens them.

And I laugh so hard my face is ugly, but defined, like the stomach of an old woman who works out a lot.

And I don't have a face, my skull has acne.

And I put my head in a fish tank and let goldfish kiss my cheeks and swim between my eyelashes and I don't take myself seriously.

And I don't want to convince you of anything.

And I hope someone reads this and commits suicide.

And I put my hands behind my back and ask you to hit me and I say, "Please, please, please hit me."

And I lie down on your carpet so long that you think I will stay forever but I get up and I see the indentation in the carpet and I get jealous and say, "I am no longer needed here."

And I have been an embarrassment to everyone I've met and I will embarrass my enemies.

And I've lived in a lot of different places and I can't make friends because I can't form feelings.

And I am an idiot and the snow stuck in your hair smells like blood.

And when my nose itches, I scratch it on the sidewalk in front of your house and then when my nose is done being itchy I look at your house and feel shitty and alone.

And if you stay quiet I will lean over and put my mouth on your neck and say hopeless things that I really mean and I'm the one with the grenade heart.

And I like juiceboxes.

And I like picking apples out of trees and eating the apples while looking at the side of your breast coming out of a sweaty shirt.

And I pull grass out of the ground and throw it into the air.

And I am quiet while you're sleeping and I blow little breaths against your hair and think, "There is a storm, and I made it."

And it seems like every moment I'm alive I'm trying to recapture something good from a long time ago and I'm walking backwards to see if that good thing comes back and tries to jump on my back for me to carry it.

And I like to carry you on my back because your sweaty vagina feels good against me.

And I am the space between your knees when you clamp them together.

And I stare at myself while brushing my teeth and I laugh because I can reproduce.

And I put my finger in the barrel of your gun and the gun explodes and black dust covers your face and you've never looked better.

And I want to sled into a tree right now and forget everything about my life so far.

And I am the homeless man walking down the street and I am holding a pillowcase full of lightbulbs and no one talks to me.

And I rarely shower and I never use deodorant and: 'Knock knock.' 'Who's there.' 'Fuck you.'

And I was raised in a womb made of taffy.

And I shaved my pubes and braided them into a rope and hanged myself from my ceiling fan.

And I am a magician: I turned my apartment into a grave.

And I get so horny sometimes that I feel like acting nice to someone.

And I set your head down on the ground and jump on it with both feet.

And I measure your smile to see if I have improved.

And I have collected my bellybutton lint for a million years and I made you a very nice sweater and I sometimes just sit on my couch, naked, wearing tennis shoes and I have hair on my chest and face and head and armpits and feet and genitals.

And I am a clown who doesn't wear makeup.

And I am the reason I know white supremacy isn't true.

And I am on two broken legs walking up concrete stairs and above each one is another one and I keep thinking I am almost done.

And I always change things and then wish I'd left them alone.

And I sit in a room that has no history.

And when you die I will not cry about it or even celebrate it; I will watch it happen and look for something else to watch.

And half of the time I am in a conversation I feel like saying, "I have nothing to say" and the other half I nod politely.

And I'm willing to sit still and hear about everything you know and I want you to show me what one minus one equals.

And I hold what is mine in my arms like I will kill to protect it.

And I never liked you.

And the ceiling looks at us like prey and I fracture my skull against a light pole and I look up at the sky and say, "Please heal me."

And when I wake up tomorrow I will finish a thought that I began when I was three.

And I saw my reflection in a lake and I waited for it to freeze a little bit so I could break it with my boot.

And I have so many hugs for everybody it just makes me want to die and the hugs are crowded in my chest and they are beginning to hate each other.

And I stand with my face very close to yours and I stop breathing so your face will stay clean.

And I will survive anything.

And I am very sick.

And I sit in the sun long enough to burn my face and I peel the flakes off and place them on peoples' tongues like the eucharist.

And I put a condom over the Sears Tower.

And I break and burn bridges between two other people and I collect the ash and make concrete for new bridges.

And I have more fun with myself than anyone else.

And I like to lie because it is fun and also because confusing people is easy and everyone is so serious and I am a transvestite clown.

And I like your hips because I can sleep with my head on them.

And I jump up and down and hope my head will hit the ceiling of the sky.

And sometimes I say mean things to people, hoping their faces will break apart like an eggshell.

And I hate your heart because it spoils you.

And I put flower petals over my tongue and lick your neck and I sew my arms to a tree.

And I will build the ugliest things on earth using the earth to build them and I sit on my front lawn with a package of waffle cones and I scoop up dirt with the waffle cones and eat dirt out of them.

And I am either a newborn baby or a very old man and I am not upset when a car splashes me, because I'm on fire.

And I know different methods of self-destruction but none as intense as sitting still by myself.

And I hope we meet again so you can guess how old I am by the rings around my eyes and I hope we meet again so I can judge how much I've died according to your limp smile.

And I wish there was a god so I could send it a note that says, "Do you like me."

And I don't like being sad sometimes.

And I think my breath is fluorescent light and I feel the sun collect in my head and explode out into new stars that everyone hates and calls ugly.

And I know there is nothing to be upset about but it feels really good to be upset.

And I have no sympathy sometimes and I argue with myself all day and I'm a used condom stuck in someone's asshole.

And I lock myself in a room and do nothing.

And my blood is red chalk and I cough it out underneath the couch.

And I sleep on my couch and wake up with grooves in my face and I press my grooved face into the mud outside and create the map to a large city.

And I step on your face while you're sleeping and while you're awake I kiss your face and I am the most selfish person alive.

And I know tonight is part of the time I worry about but it is different because I use it to worry about what's coming and I know that what's coming is almost always disastrous and I say that the next day will be different but then end up doing nothing to effect that change.

And I want everyone to hate me because then I work best.

And I draw all the people I know on a chalkboard and sit by the chalkboard crossing them off one by one and I cover my hands with cellophane so nothing remembers me.

And I remember me better than anyone.

And I remember you how I need to and I am the old man sitting alone on a bench at the park looking at a newspaper but not really reading it.

And I trap bugs and then let them go.

And I say, "Peek-a-boo" and throw a knife at your house.

And I never say I'm sorry.

And I break my nose for something to do and I dig small holes and plant crayons and watch beams of color puncture the sky and I strangle you while you sleep.

And I threaten my neighbors with dirt smeared on my face and I bite off a fingernail and spit it into a spiderweb.

And, surprise, I like you way more than a friend.

And I rip out my tongue and put it in your belly and you starve to death.

And I am the best person ever and I hate everything I see.

And I dress up like a woman and jump from a tree and break my neck and lie there until the sun goes down and animals emerge and eat me.

And I cinch a belt around my head and crush my skull and use the pieces to pick my teeth.

And I talk until my mouth is dry and then I keep talking through the dry-choking.

And I buried an eyelash in drying concrete and I cut my finger on a book at the library and surprise now I'm immortal.

And I think about how tomorrow will be over soon enough and then I'll point at it and laugh at everything that happened.

PLEASE

Put your mouth around my ear so it sounds like I'm drowning in the ocean.

HARDCORE SEX

I used to work as a house painter. One time, I cut my knuckles open while scraping a window. The daughter of the guy who owned the house, she took me inside when I asked her for a band-aid. She washed my hand in the sink and then put a band-aid over the knuckles. We didn't talk at all. I kept my eyes on the blood going down the drain. I felt like a monster from some generic fairy-tale idea, like where a pretty girl helps out the monster because she feels bad for it and then the townspeople find out and hunt the monster.

A VERY SHORT PLAY

A man and a woman are in bed in a room that is dark blue because the sun is setting. Water is hitting the window.

WOMAN: [looking out the window] Oh shit, it's raining again.

MAN: No.

WOMAN: [turns] What do you mean? I can see it.

MAN: Uh, I just set up the sprinkler while you were sleeping so the spray would hit the window. I didn't want you to leave.

I AM A CHAMPION AND YOU ARE THE ECHO OF MY LAST BREATH

When I was nine, I saw my neighbor's breasts. I was in my backyard hitting fireflies with a waffle bat. She was twelve at the time. She came outside and joined me. I continued to hit fireflies. She kept trying to tell me about her goldfish. I ignored her. Eventually, she ran across the yard and did a cartwheel. Her shirt crumpled up, revealing two immature breasts. They were mostly nipple, each nipple the color of an old pear. I hit a firefly to the ground and watched the light in its belly fade. Then I went inside and masturbated like I was a gold medal masturbator masturbating at the masturbation Olympics.

I CLIPPED A RANDOM PICTURE FROM AN OBITUARY AND THEN ATE IT, HOPING I'D GIVE BIRTH TO THE REINCARNATED BODY OF THE PERSON IN THE PICTURE, BUT I DIDN'T, I JUST SHIT OUT THE PICTURE

I am going to clone myself then kill the clone and eat it.

I just reversed all your ceremonies—how do you feel.

I threw everything my throat had into the center of your mouth and turned your teeth into a broken and mud-splashed fence. You ate it like a greedy weakling. You make me hard.

In lieu of a condom I used a thoroughly chewed piece of raspberry gum when I fucked that dead moose over there (yes, that one over there, the one with the raspberry-smelling genitalia, no, over one, over one—yep, that one there.)

Goddamn, I have no feelings and the lines around my face already need to be cleaned again. I am a greedy weakling and I make myself hard.

I just reversed all your ceremonies again—that makes them the same as before.

I can trace my bloodline back to a stone at the bottom of the Atlantic Ocean and you know what, the best time to throw a lit match into someone's mouth is when they're laughing.

Light the wick that connects to the veins attached to your heart. When you explode, the pieces of your body and your blood will line the wall. And I'll press my finger into the gore when it congeals so it will hold the impress of my fingerprint until the end of time when the lake in space eats the sun and everyone acts like there's a god, making sense of their real hero: themselves.

It's hard to determine if the emotion I'm feeling is mine or coming from somewhere.

For the past few hours I couldn't stop thinking about how it's impossible to sense my own weight so I thought about it and even tried lifting my arm and leg and other various parts but I was always right there.

The revenge of earth is reproduction.

It's killing me.

Actually no, my life never really got started.

I am going to board a freight train and it will take me somewhere that is not here. When it stops I will get off and look around and smile. It will be where I'm supposed to be.

ALZHEIMER'S DISEASE

When I get to hell I will save you a seat.

When you get to hell I will act like I don't know you.

BEING ALONE ISN'T BAD
ONCE YOU REALIZE
NO ONE HAS ANYTHING
TO OFFER YOU

Some girl at a New Year's Eve party offered to show me her breasts for a quarter. I had the quarter but refused her. Then I explained to her that I needed the quarter to buy a gumball on my way home. She was angry. I bought the gumball and chewed it until all the flavor was gone.

SOMETHING I WORRY ABOUT

Walking home yesterday, I went between two streetlights. I watched the shadow in front of me and the one behind me move and align perfectly beneath. I worry that I am never going to learn anything or have anything important to say.

LET'S GO ON A DATE TOGETHER

Hello I am waiting in the parking garage for you and I have a bouquet of arm bones. Would you like to go on a date with me. You'll have to pay because I'm broke. Or we can go to my place instead. And I can comb your hair with the stem of a rose. And make faces behind your back. Turn you around and hug you. And slowly slip a knife through your back so it comes out the front and pierces me and we die connected.

ON OUR DATE

We were at my apartment watching tv.

I took a tray of brownies out of the oven and cut one and joined you in the livingroom.

"Open your mouth," I said. "I have a nice brownie for you."

I waved the brownie in front of your face.

You smiled and I touched your nose lightly with my finger like your nose was a button and I was trying to activate something.

You took the brownie.

"Excuse me," I said. "I have to use the bathroom."

You smiled at me as I walked up the stairs.

In the bathroom, I brushed my teeth so my breath would smell good.

I also put water on my face and washed my hands.

Then I went back downstairs.

You were watching a television show where a large group of

people compete for the love of one person.

The doorbell rang.

I tapped your shoulder gently and got up to answer the door.

You grabbed my arm and made your lips into a kissing shape.

You pointed at your lips.

I leaned down and kissed you.

When I answered the door, it was the mailman.

He handed me a few letters then looked around.

He pulled his bag forward and reached in.

"Here you go," he said quietly.

He handed me a small, greasy object.

I looked at it.

It was a dead bird, covered in ink.

The feathers were sticking up and the beak was open.

The ink ran over my palm and wrist and through my fingers.

"I made it myself," the mailman said.

Then he winked and backed away.

I closed the door and looked at the bird.

The sound from the television came around the hall and I heard people fighting.

I returned to the couch and you put your head down on my lap.

I held the bird in my hands and watched the ink drop into my lap and onto your face.

I AM THE LAWNMOWER

Until I die, the world is the yard, composed of hands reaching up to shake mine.

And I am the lawnmower.

I LOVE YOU, YOU SHITHEAD

When I touch my face to yours, I think, "This is our first mistake."

I'M A NEGATIVE ASSHOLE AND THE EARTH IS A STUPID PLANET THAT SUPPORTS THE WEIGHT OF ITS OWN DESTRUCTION

Boo hoo. I am so sad.

I am in my room with the door locked, anticipating death.

There is no one in my room but me, and I am no one.

And I will welcome in whatever kills me.

The earth is stupid.

It is the only planet that supports the weight of its own destruction.

I am a negative asshole and the earth is stupid.

It supports me and I am ungrateful.

I will give the earth an unnecessary c-section and jump into the wound.

The earth will become sick with my body.

It will welcome in the thing that kills it.

Boo hoo. That makes me so sad.

I want to lie in the street and get run over repeatedly.

I want to put matches underneath my eyelids and blink tiny flames at someone.

I am a negative asshole.

And your crying is a song to me.

I will dismember everyone and sew millions of arms together to make a flag.

Then wave the flag over the sun and everything will change color.

Earth is stupid.

I will burn it down.

Then blacken my face with the ash.

Boo hoo. I am so sad.

And I think that anyone who likes me doesn't know everything they need to know.

Sit alone when you are happy. That way it won't spread.

Cry into a bottle and put a rag in the bottle and light the rag on fire then throw it at the sky. The sky will melt and drown us.

This is the captain.

I have made a home on a stupid planet.

Whoever runs my brain is doing a shitty job.

And I support the weight of my own destruction.

The way home is beneath your feet.

The way home is to drop dead.

And be done.

I don't have any feelings and your crying is a song to me.

I want to sit and watch you cry.

I'm like reverse-god.

And I'll give you an unnecessary c-section.

And my hands won't hate their work.

Like reverse-god.

And I'm in my room, slowly becoming garbage.

My cum smells like flower compost.

And it is in you.

And you are a skeleton.

And my cum makes holes in your skeleton.

And you support the weight of your own destruction.

You slowly die.

And my hands don't hate their work.

Welcome in whatever kills you.

Sit alone in your room with your door locked.

Anticipating death.

Sit alone. And welcome in whatever kills you.

The way home is to drop dead.

And be done.

Boo hoo. That makes me sad.

THE WORST PART ABOUT ANYTHING
IS THAT IT WILL BE OVER

I am going to cook my hand over the burner on the stove and eat all the meat off, leaving only the bone. Then I am going to pin my skeleton hand against the ground with my knee and break it off at the forearm. I am going to take the skeleton hand outside and stick it into the ground, planting a different kind of flower. Still waving, still eating sun. This is saying goodbye. I am going.

DEAD HORSE

If I ever find a dead horse, I am going to beat the fucking shit out of it. I will beat the shit out of the dead horse until all the bones in my fingers, hands, wrists and arms are broken. Then I will beat the dead horse with my feet and let my broken arms flail uncontrollably like a violent sprinkler. If I ever find a dead horse, I am going to beat the fucking shit out of it.

ABOUT THE AUTHOR

SAM PINK is the author of *The No Hellos Diet*, *Hurt Others*, *No One Can Do Anything Worse to You Than You Can*, *Frowns Need Friends Too*, and the cult hit *Person*. His writing has been published widely in print and on the internet, and also in other languages. He lives in Chicago, where he plays in the band Depressed Woman.

Be his friend at impersonalelectroniccommunication.com.

CPSIA information can be obtained at www.ICGtesting.com
Printed in the USA
LVOW121218021212

309701LV00005B/809/P